Charles Martel

Charles Martel
The Military Leader and Frankish Defender

Collection

© *LM Publishers*

"Charles Martel defeated the Moslem army effectively ending Moslem attempts to conquer western Europe."

- *Dictionary of Battles*

Chapter I [1]

Charles Martel is generally considered as the Frankish Military Leader who defeated the Moslem army and stopped the great movement of Arab conquest in Europe. His victory during the battle of Tours (also called the battle of Poitiers) is described by the historians as the decisive event which preserved the European Civilization.

According to E. Gibbon the victory of Charles Martel rescued the ancestors of *Europeans*, from the Islamic civilization. And the historian L. Von Ranke said : "the battle of Poitiers was the turning point of

---

[1] Based on the works of Christian Pfister; John H. Haaren. See the detail of the bibliography at the end of the book.

one of the most important epochs in the history of the world."

Who was really Charles Martel?

Before to present his life and actions, here are some interesting events in the history :

I

In 711 the Arabs had conquered Spain. In 720 they crossed the Pyrenees, seized Narbonensis, a dependency of the kingdom of the Visigoths, and advanced on Gaul. By his able policy Odo succeeded in arresting their progress for some years; but a new vali, Abdur Rahman, a member of an extremely fanatical sect, resumed the attack, reached Poitiers, and advanced on Tours, the holy town of Gaul.

In October 732 - just 100 years after the death of Mahomet – Charles Martel gained a brilliant victory over Abdur Rahman, who was called back to Africa by the revolts of the Berbers and had to give up the struggle. This was the last of the great Arab invasions of Europe.

About the history of the Arab conquest and their defeat at Tours, R. M. Johnston wrote :

The fanaticized hosts of Arabia and the East were knocking at the gates of Constantinople, and swept westward along the southern shores of the Mediterranean until the Atlantic barred their steps. They turned to Spain, destroyed the Visigothic kingdom, crossed the Pyrenees, and reached the center of Gaul before they were at last checked. The Franks under Charles Martel defeated them, and perhaps by that victory saved Christendom. Had the Arabs succeeded in this last ordeal, who knows what the result might not have been?

After his victory Charles took the offensive, and endeavoured to wrest Narbonensis from the Muslims. Although he was not successful in his attempt to recover Narbonne (737), he destroyed the fortresses of Agde, Béziers and Maguelonne, and set fire to the amphitheatre at Nîmes. He subdued also the Germanic tribes; annexed Frisia, where Christianity was beginning to make progress; put an end to the duchy of Alemannia; intervened in the internal affairs of the dukes of Bavaria; made expeditions into Saxony; and in 738 compelled some of the Saxon tribes to pay him tribute. He also gave St Boniface a safe conduct for his missions in Thuringia, Alemannia and Bavaria.

E. Gibbon wrote : "A victorious line of march had been prolonged above a thousand miles from the rock of Gibraltar to the banks of the Loire; the repetition of an equal space would have carried the Saracens to the confines of Poland and the Highlands of Scotland; the Rhine is not more impassable than the Nile or Euphrates, and the Arabian fleet might have sailed without a naval combat into the mouth of the Thames. Perhaps the interpretation of the Koran would now be taught in the schools of Oxford and her pulpits might demonstrate to a circumcised people the sanctity and truth of the revelation of Mahomet."

II

After the death of Mohammed the Saracens, also called Mohammedans, are became great warriors. They conquered many countries and established the Mohammedan religion in them.

In 711, when they intended to conquer the land of the Franks, and then all Europe, they thought it would be easy, because the Frankish king at that time was a very weak man. He was one of a number of kings who were called the "Do-nothings." They reigned from about 638 to 751. They spent all their time in amusements and pleasures, leaving the affairs of the government to be managed by persons called Mayors of the Palace.

Strauss G. L[2]. wrote:

When the Roman Empire had ceased to exist, the Frankish kings had, in imitation of the Roman rulers, begun to surround themselves with a court, and a great many high officers, and charges had been created, among the most important of which may be mentioned the office of Lord High Chancellor; Lord High Chamberlain, or High Treasurer; Master of the royal stables; Lord Justice; Steward of the royal household; and more particularly that of Mayor of the palace.

The functions of the latter officer had originally been confined to the general superintendence of the palace, and the administration of the royal domains; but had speedily been extended also to the

---

[2] in *Charles Martel and the Rescue of Europe from the threatened yoke of the Saracens.*

command of the household troops. In the course of the domestic wars between the Merovingian princes, the mayors of the palace had gradually acquired a power and influence second only to that of the king.

The mayors of the palace were officers who at first managed the king's household. Afterwards they were made guardians of kings who came to the throne when very young. So long as the king was under age the mayor of the palace acted as chief officer of the government in his name. And as several of the young kings, even when they were old enough to rule, gave less attention to business than to pleasure, the mayors continued to do all the business, until at last they did everything that the king ought to have done. They made war, led armies in battle, raised money and spent it, and carried on the government as they pleased, without consulting the king.

The "Do-nothings" had the title of king, but nothing more. In fact, they did not desire to have any business to do. The things they cared for were dogs, horses and sport.

One of the most famous of the mayors was a man named Pepin. Once a year, it is said, Pepin had the king dressed in his finest clothes and paraded through the city of Paris, where the court was held. A splendid throng of nobles and courtiers accompanied the king, and did him honor as he went along the streets in a gilded chariot drawn by a long line of beautiful horses. The king was cheered by the people, and he acknowledged their greetings most graciously.

After the parade the king was escorted to the great hall of the palace, which was filled with nobles. Seated on a magnificent throne, he saluted the assemblage and made a short speech. The speech was prepared beforehand by Pepin, and committed to memory by the king. At the close of the ceremony the royal "nobody" retired to his country house and was not heard of again for a year.

Chapter II [3]

General History of Charles Martel

I

Born about 688 and died in 741; Charles Martel was the natural son of Pepin of Herstal and a woman named Alpaïde or Chalpaïde.

Pepin had outlived his two legitimate sons, Drogon and Grimoald, and to Theodoald, a son of the latter and then only six years old, fell the burdensome inheritance of the French monarchy. Charles, who was then twenty-six, was not excluded from the succession on account of his birth, Theodoald himself being the

---

[3] Based on the work of Strauss G. L., Godefroid Kurth

son of a concubine, but through the influence of Plectrude, Theodoald's grandmother, who wished the power invested in her own descendants exclusively. To prevent any opposition from Charles she had him cast into prison and, having established herself at Cologne, assumed the guardianship of her grandson. But the different nations whom the strong hand of Pepin of Herstal had held in subjections, shook off the yoke of oppression as soon as they saw that it was with a woman they had to deal. Neustria gave the signal for revolt (715), Theodoald was beaten in the forest of Cuise and, led by Raginfrid, mayor of the palace, the enemy advanced as far as the Meuse. The Frisians flew to arms and, headed by their duke, Ratbod, destroyed the Christian mission and entered into a confederacy with the Neustrians. The Saxons came and devastated the country of the Hattuarians, and even in Austrasia there was a certain faction that chafed under the government of a woman and child. At this juncture Charles escaped from prison and put himself at the head of the national party of Austrasia. At first he was unfortunate. He was defeated by Ratbod near Cologne in 716, and the Neustrians forced Plectrude to acknowledge as king Chilperic, the son of Childeric II, having taken this Merovingian from the seclusion of the cloister, where he lived the name of Daniel. But Charles was quick to take revenge. He surprised and conquered the Neustrians at Amblève near Malmédy (716), defeated them a second time at Vincy near Cambrai (21 March,

717), and pursued them as far as Paris. Then retracing his steps, he came to Cologne and compelled Plectrude to surrender her power and turn over to him the wealth of his father, Pepin. In order to give his recently acquired authority a semblance of legitimacy, he proclaimed the Merovingian Clotaire IV King of Austrasia, reserving for himself the title of Mayor of the Palace. It was about this time that Charles banished Rigobert, the Bishop of Reims, who had opposed him, appointing in his stead the warlike and unpriestly Milon, who was already Archbishop of Trier.

The ensuing years were full of strife. Eager to chastise the Saxons who had invaded Austrasia, Charles in the year 718 laid waste their country to the banks of the Weser.

In 719 Ratbod died, and Charles seized Western Friesland without any great resistance on the part of the Frisians, who had taken possession of it on the death of Pepin.

The Neustrians, always a menace, had joined forces with the people of Aquitaine, but Charles hacked their army to pieces at Soissons. After this defeat they realized the necessity of surrendering, and the death of King Clotaire IV, whom Charles had placed on the throne but two years previously, facilitated reconciliation of the two great fractions of the Frankish Empire. Charles acknowledged Chilperic as head of the entire monarchy, while on their side, the Neustrians and Aquitainians endorsed the authority of Charles; but, when Chilperic died, the following year (720) Charles appointed as his successor the son of Dagobert III, Thierry IV, who was still a minor, and who occupied the throne from 720 to 737.

A second expedition against the Saxons in 720 and the definitive submission of Raginfrid, who had been left the county of Angers (724), re-established the Frankish Monarchy as it had been under Pepin of Herstal, and closed the first series of Charles Martel's struggles.

The next six years were devoted almost exclusively to the confirming of the Frankish authority over the dependent Germanic tribes.

In 725 and 728 Charles went into Bavaria, where the Agilolfing dukes had gradually rendered themselves independent, and re-established Frankish suzerainty. He also brought thence the Princess Suanehilde, who seems to have become his mistress.

In 730 he marched against Lantfrid, Duke of the Alemanna, whom he likewise brought into subjection, and thus Southern Germany once more became part of the Frankish Empire, as had Northern Germany during the first years of the reign. But at the extremity of the empire a dreadful storm was gathering. For several years the Moslems of Spain had been threatening Gaul. Banished thence in 721 by Duke Eudes, they had returned in 725 and penetrated as far as Burgundy, where they had destroyed Autun. Duke Eudes, unable to resist them, at length contented himself by negotiating with them, and to Othmar, one of their chiefs, he gave the hand of his daughter But this compromising alliance brought him into disfavour with Charles, who defeated him in 731, and the death of Othmar that same year again left Eudes at the mercy of Moslem enterprise.

In 732 Abd-er-Rahman, Governor of Spain, crossed the Pyrenees at the head of an immense army, overcame Duke Eudes, and advanced as far as the Loire, pillaging and burning as he went. In October, 732, Charles met Abd-er-Rahman outside of Tours and defeated and slew him in a battle (the Battle of Poitiers) which must ever remain one of the great events in the history of the world, as upon its issue depended whether Christian Civilization should continue or Islam prevail throughout Europe. It was this battle, it is said, that gave Charles his name, *Martel* (*Tudites*) "The Hammer", because of the merciless way in which he smote the enemy.

The remainder of Charles Martel's reign was an uninterrupted series of triumphant combats.

In 733-734 he suppressed the rebellion instigated by the Frisian duke, Bobo, who was slain in battle, and definitively subdued Friesland, which finally adopted Christianity.

In 735, after the death of Eudes, Charles entered Aquitaine, quelled the revolt of

Hatto and Hunold, sons of the deceased duke, and left the duchy to Hunold, to be held in fief (736). He then banished the Moslems from Arles and Avignon, defeated their army on the River Berre near Narbonne, and in 739 checked an uprising in Provence, the rebels being under the leadership of Maurontus. So great was Charles' power during the last years of his reign that he did not take the trouble to appoint a successor to King Thierry IV, who died in 737, but assumed full authority himself, governing without legal right. About a year before Charles died, Pope Gregory III, threatened by Luitprand, King of Lombardy, asked his help.

Now Charles was Luitprand's ally because the latter had promised to assist him in the late war against the Moslems of

Provence, and, moreover, the Frankish king may have already suffered from the malady that was to carry him off-two reasons that are surely sufficient to account for the fact that the pope's envoys departed without gaining the object of their errand. However, it would seem that, according to the terms of a public act published by Charlemagne, Charles had, at least in principle, agreed to defend the Roman Church, and death alone must have prevented him from fulfilling this agreement.

The reign, which in the beginning was so full of bloody conflicts and later of such incessant strife, would have been an impossibility had not Charles procured means sufficient to attract and compensate his partisans. For this purpose he conceived the idea of giving them the usufruct of a great many ecclesiastical lands, and this spoliation is what is referred to as the secularization by Charles Martel. It was an expedient that could be excused without, however, being justified, and it was pardoned to a certain extent by the amnesty granted at the Council of Lestines, held under the sons of Charles Martel in 743. It must also be remembered that the Church remained the legal owner of the lands thus alienated. This spoliation and the conferring of the principal ecclesiastical dignities upon those who were either totally unworthy or else had naught but their military qualifications to recommend them-as, for instance, the assignment of the episcopal Sees of Reims of Reims and Trier to Milon-were not calculated to endear Charles Martel to the clergy of his time. Therefore, in the ninth century Hincmar of Reims related the story of the vision with which St. Eucher was said to have been favoured and which showed Charles in hell, to which he had been condemned for robbing the Church of its property.

But notwithstanding the almost exclusively warlike character of his reign, Charles Martel was not indifferent to the superior interests of civilization and Christianity.

Like Napoleon after the French Revolution, upon emerging from the years 715-719, Charles, who had not only tolerated but perpetrated many an act of violence against the Church, set about the establishment of social order and endeavoured to restore the rights of the Catholic hierarchy. This explains the protection which in 723 he accorded St. Boniface (Winfrid), the great apostle of Germany, a protection all the more salutary as the saint himself explained to his old friend, Daniel of Winchester, that without it he could neither administer his church, defend his clergy, nor prevent idolatry. Hence Charles Martel shares, to a certain degree, the glory and merit of Boniface's great work of civilization. He died after having divided the Frankish Empire, as a patrimony between his two sons, Carloman and Pepin.

II [4]

Charles Martel had two sons, Pepin and Carloman. For a time they ruled together, but Carloman wished to lead a religious life, so he went to a monastery and became a monk. Then Pepin was sole ruler.

Pepin was quite low in stature, and therefore was called Pepin the Short. But he had great strength and courage. A story is told of him, which shows how fearless he was.

One day he went with a few of his nobles to a circus to see a fight between a lion and a bull. Soon after the fight began, it looked as though the bull was getting the worst of it. Pepin cried out to his companions:

---

[4] Based on the work of John H. Haaren.

"Will one of you separate the beasts?"

But there was no answer. None of them had the courage to make the attempt. Then Pepin jumped from his seat, rushed into the arena, and with a thrust of his sword killed the lion.

In the early years of Pepin's rule as mayor of the palace the throne was occupied by a king named Childeric III. Like his father and the other "do-nothing" kings, Childeric cared more for pleasures and amusements than for affairs of government. Pepin was the real ruler, and after a while he began to think that he ought to have the title of king, as he had all the power and did all the work of governing and defending the kingdom.

So he sent some friends to Rome to consult the Pope. They said to His Holiness:

"Holy father, who ought to be the king of France—the man who has the title, or the man who has the power and does all the duties of king?"

"Certainly," replied the Pope, "the man who has the power and does the duties."

"Then, surely," said they, "Pepin ought to be the king of the Franks; for he has all the power."

The Pope gave his consent, and Pepin was crowned king of the Franks; and thus the reign of Childeric ended and that of Pepin began.

During nearly his whole reign Pepin was engaged in war. Several times he went to

Italy to defend the Pope against the Lombards. These people occupied certain parts of Italy, including the province still called Lombardy.

Pepin conquered them and gave as a present to the Pope that part of their possessions which extended for some distance around Rome. This was called "Pepin's Donation." It was the beginning of what is known as the "temporal power" of the Popes, that is, their power as rulers of part of Italy.

Some Interesting Dates:

In 722, Charles Martel drove the Saxons from the Hassian (Hessian) district which they had invaded; but when he followed them into their own country, with the intention of subjecting them altogether to his sway, he experienced such determined resistance that he wisely resolved to leave them alone.

In 725, he compelled the Suabians and Alemanni, and their duke, Lantfried, to acknowledge his sovereignty.

Since 553, after the extinction of the Gothic kingdom of Italy, the Agilolfingian dukes of Bavaria "enjoyed" the "protection" of the Frankish kings; although, whenever the dissensions among the members of that amiable family, or the contentions among the mayors of the palace, afforded a fitting opportunity, the Bavarians invariably took occasion to "thank" them for their protection, and to decline further favors. But the persuasive force of Pepin of Heristal, and of his son Charles, fully succeeded in the end in restoring the amicable relations between the two nations, to the old footing. Duke Theodo II., a most pious prince, who greatly favored and farthered the extension of Christianity in his dominions, committed the capital blunder 80 common at the time (and so natural withal) — to divide his dominions between his three sons, Theodoald (Theudebaud), Theudebert, and Grimoald. Theudebaud had married Pilitrudis, the fair daughter of

Plectrudis ; he died in 716, and his brother Grimoald deemed it no harm to marry the beautiful widow of the departed; but Saint Corbinian happened to think very differently ; and his zealous exhortations, and the fearful picture which he drew of the pains and penalties that awaited him who should have committed, what the holy man was pleased to call, "incest", frightened poor Duke Grimoald into giving his consent to a divorce from his dearly beloved wife. Mistress Pilitrudis, however, was by no means pleased with the pusillanimous conduct of her second husband; and the exile of the meddlesome ecclesiastic speedily showed him, that a woman offended may prove more than a match even for a priest and a saint. Theudebert also died (724), leaving behind a son, named Hugibert, and a daughter, named Guntrudis, and who was married to Liutprand, King of the Lombards. After his second brother's death, Grimoald seized upon his dominions to the prejudice of his nephew. Hugibert, finding all his remonstrances disregarded, claimed the intercession of the Duke of the Franks, in his capacity as Protector of Bavaria.

Charles accepted the offer of mediator between the contending parties; and called upon Grimoald to deliver up to Hugibert the provinces which he was unjustly withholding from him. Grimoald refusing, Charles entered Bavaria at the head of his army, and the Bavarian duke was defeated and slain in the first battle (725). Hugibert now succeeded to the government of all Bavaria, with the exception, however, of a large slice of the Northern provinces, which he ceded to Charles in reward of his services. The unfortunate Pilitrudis was despoiled by the "magnanimous" victor of all she possessed, except a mule, or donkey, to carry her to Pavia to her relations. A new irruption of the Saxons, called Charles again to the Weser; he defeated and drove back the invaders (729). Whilst he was thus occupied on the Saxon frontier, the Suabians and Alemanni took advantage of his absence, to throw off once more the yoke of the Franks. Charles Martel confounded them, however, by the rapidity of his movements; he appeared on the Mein before they were well aware that he had left the banks of the Weser. The battle which ensued, terminated in the total defeat of the "rebels; Duke Lantfried was slain, and the humbled nation submitted to the rule of the conqueror (730).

Chapter III

The Battle of Tours (in 732) [5]

The broad tract of Champaign country which intervenes between the cities of Poitiers and Tours is principally composed of a succession of rich pasture lands, which are traversed and fertilized by the Cher, the Creuse, the Vienne, the Claine, the Indre, and other tributaries of the river Loire. Here and there, the ground swells into picturesque eminences; and occasionally a belt of forest land, a brown heath, or a clustering series of vineyards, breaks the monotony of the wide-spread meadows; but the general character of the land is that

---

[5] Based on the work of Edward Shepherd Creasy in *The Fifteen Decisive Battles of the World.*

of a grassy plain, and it seems naturally adapted for the evolutions of numerous armies, especially of those vast bodies of cavalry which, principally decided the fate of nations during the centuries that followed the downfall of Rome, and preceded the consolidation of the modern European powers.

This region has been signalized by more than one memorable conflict; but it is principally interesting to the historian, by having been the scene of the great victory won by Charles Martel over the Saracens, A.D. 732, which gave a decisive check to the career of Arab conquest in Western Europe, rescued Christendom from Islam, preserved the relics of ancient and the germs of modern civilization, and re-established the old superiority of the Indo-

European over the Semitic family of mankind.

Sismondi and Michelet have underrated the enduring interest of this great Appeal of Battle between the champions of the Crescent and the Cross. But, if French writers have slighted the exploits of their national hero, the Saracenic trophies of Charles Martel have had full justice done to them by English and German historians. Gibbon devotes several pages of his great work to the narrative of the battle of Tours, and to the consideration of the consequences which probably would have resulted, if Abderrahman's enterprise had not been crushed by the Frankish chief. Schlegel speaks of this "mighty victory" in terms of fervent gratitude; and tells how "the arms of Charles Martel saved and delivered the Christian nations of the West from the deadly grasp of all-destroying Islam"; and Ranke points out, as "one of the most important epochs in the history of the world, the commencement of the eighth century; when, on the one side, Mahommedanism threatened to overspread Italy and Gaul, and on the other, the ancient idolatry of Saxony and Friesland once more forced its way across the Rhine. In this peril of Christian institutions, a youthful prince of Germanic race, Karl Martell, arose as their champion; maintained them with all the energy which the necessity for self-defense calls forth, and finally extended them into new regions."

Arnold ranks the victory of Charles Martel even higher than the victory of

Arminius, "among those signal deliverances which have affected for centuries the happiness of mankind."

In fact, the more we test its importance, the higher we shall be led to estimate it; and, though the authentic details which we possess of its circumstances and its heroes are but meagre, we can trace enough of its general character to make us watch with deep interest this encounter between the rival conquerors of the decaying Roman empire. That old classic world, the history of which occupies so large a portion of our early studies, lay, in the eighth century of our era, utterly exanimate and overthrown.

On the north the German, on the south the Arab, was rending away its provinces. At last the spoilers encountered one another, each striving for the full mastery of the prey. Their conflict brought back upon the memory of Gibbon the old Homeric simile, where the strife of Hector and Patroclus over the dead body of Cebriones is compared to the combat of two lions, that in their hate and hunger fight together on the mountain-tops over the carcass of a slaughtered stag: and the reluctant yielding of the Saracen power to the superior might of the Northern warriors, might not inaptly recall those other lines of the same book of the Iliad, where the downfall of Patroclus beneath Hector is likened to the forced yielding of the panting and exhausted wild boar, that had long and furiously fought with a superior beast of prey for the possession of the fountain among the rocks, at which each burned to drink.

Although three centuries had passed away since the Germanic conquerors of Rome had crossed the Rhine, never to repass that frontier stream, no settled system of institutions or government, no amalgamation of the various races into one people, no uniformity of language or habits, had been established in the country, at the time when Charles Martel was called on to repel the menacing tide of Saracenic invasion from the south.

Gaul was not yet France. In that, as in other provinces of the Roman empire of the West, the dominion of the Caesars had been shattered as early as the fifth century, and barbaric kingdoms and principalities had promptly arisen on the ruins of the Roman power. But few of these had any permanency; and none of them consolidated the rest, or any considerable number of the rest, into one coherent and organized civil and political society.

The great bulk of the population still consisted of the conquered provincials, that is to say, of Romanized Celts, of a Gallic race which had long been under the dominion of the Caesars, and had acquired, together with no slight infusion of Roman blood, the language, the literature, the laws, and the civilization of Latium.

Among these, and dominant over them, roved or dwelt the German victors: some retaining nearly all the rude independence of their primitive national character; others, softened and disciplined by the aspect and contact of the manners and institutions of civilized life. For it is to be borne in mind, that the Roman empire in the West was not crushed by any sudden avalanche of barbaric invasion.

The German conquerors came across the Rhine, not in enormous hosts, but in bands of a few thousand warriors at a time. The conquest of a province was the result of an infinite series of partial local invasions, carried on by little armies of this description.

The victorious warriors either retired with their booty, or fixed themselves in the invaded district, taking care to keep sufficiently concentrated for military purposes, and ever ready for some fresh foray, either against a rival Teutonic band, or some hitherto unassailed city of the provincials.

Gradually, however, the conquerors acquired a desire for permanent landed possessions. They lost somewhat of the restless thirst for novelty and adventure which had first made them throng beneath the banner of the boldest captains of their tribe, and leave their native forests for a roving military Life on the left bank of the Rhine. They were converted to the Christian faith; and gave up with their old creed much of the coarse ferocity, which must have been fostered in the spirits of the ancient warriors of the North by a mythology which promised, as the reward of the brave on earth, an eternal cycle of fighting and drunkenness in heaven.

But, although their conversion and other civilizing influences operated powerfully upon the Germans in Gaul; and although the Franks (who were originally a confederation of the Teutonic tribes that dwelt between the Rhine, the Maine, and the Weser) established a decided superiority over the other conquerors of the province, as well as over the conquered provincials, the country long remained a chaos of uncombined and shifting elements.

The early princes of the Merovingian dynasty were generally occupied in wars against other princes of their house, occasioned by the frequent subdivisions of the Frank monarchy: and the ablest and best of them had found all their energies tasked to the utmost to defend the barrier of the Rhine against the Pagan Germans, who strove to pass that river and gather their share of the spoils of the empire.

The conquests which the Saracens effected over the southern and eastern provinces of Rome were far more rapid than those achieved by the Germans in the north; and the new organizations of society which the Moslems introduced were summarily and uniformly enforced. Exactly a century passed between the death of Mohammed and the date of the battle of Tours.

During that century the followers of the Prophet had torn away half the Roman empire; and besides their conquests over

Persia, the Saracens had overrun Syria, Egypt, Africa, and Spain, in an unchequered and apparently irresistible career of victory. Nor, at the commencement of the eighth century of our era, was the Mohammedan world divided against itself, as it subsequently became. All these vast regions obeyed the Caliph; throughout them all, from the Pyrenees to the Oxus, the name of Mohammed was invoked in prayer, and the Koran revered as the book of the law.

It was under one of their ablest and most renowned commanders, with a veteran army, and with every apparent advantage of time, place, and circumstance, that the Arabs made their great effort at the conquest of Europe north of the Pyrenees. The victorious Moslem soldiery in Spain,

"A countless multitude;

Syrian, Moor, Saracen, Greek renegade,
Persian, and Copt, and Tartar, in one bond
Of erring faith conjoined--strong in the youth

And heat of zeal--a dreadful brotherhood,"

were eager for the plunder of more Christian cities and shrines, and full of fanatic confidence in the invincibility of their arms.

"Nor were the chiefs

Of victory less assured, by long success
Elate, and proud of that o'erwhelming strength
Which surely, they believed, as it had rolled
Thus far uncheck'd, would roll victorious on,
Till, like the Orient, the subjected West
Should bow in reverence at Mahommed's name;
And pilrims from remotest Arctic shores
Tread with religious feet the burning sands
Of Araby and Mecca's stony soil."

Southey's Roderick.

It is not only by the modern Christian poet, but by the old Arabian chroniclers also, that these feelings of ambition and arrogance are attributed to the Moslems, who had overthrown the Visigoth power in Spain. And their eager expectations of new wars were excited to the utmost on the re-appointment by the Caliph of Abderrahman Ibn Abdillah Alghafeki to the government of that country, A.D. 729, which restored them a general who had signalized his skill and prowess during the conquests of Africa and Spain, whose ready valour and generosity had made him the idol of the troops, who had already been engaged in several expeditions into Gaul, so as to be well acquainted with the national character and tactics of the Franks; and who was known to thirst, like a good

Moslem, for revenge for the slaughter of some detachments of the true believers, which had been cut off on the north of the Pyrenees.

In addition to his cardinal military virtues, Abderrahman is described by the Arab writers as a model of integrity and justice.

The first two years of his second administration in Spain were occupied in severe reforms of the abuses which under his predecessors had crept into the system of government, and in extensive preparations for his intended conquest of Gaul. Besides the troops which he collected from his province, he obtained from Africa a large body of chosen Barber cavalry, officered by Arabs of proved skill and valour: and in the summer of 732 he crossed the Pyrenees at the head of an army which some Arab writers rate at eighty thousand strong, while some of the Christian chroniclers swell its numbers to many hundreds of thousands more. Probably the Arab account diminishes, but of the two keeps nearer to the truth. It was from this formidable host, after Eudes, the Count of Acquitaine, had vainly striven to check it, after many strong cities had fallen before it, and half the land been overrun, that Gaul and Christendom were at last rescued by the strong arm of Prince Charles, who acquired a surname, like that of the war-god of his forefathers' creed, from the might with which he broke and shattered his enemies in the battle.

The Merovingian kings had sunk into absolute insignificance, and had become mere puppets of royalty before the eighth century. Charles Martel like his father, Pepin Heristal, was Duke of the Austrasian Franks, the bravest and most thoroughly Germanic part of the nation: and exercised, in the name of the titular king, what little paramount authority the turbulent minor rulers of districts and towns could be persuaded or compelled to acknowledge. Engaged with his national competitors in perpetual conflicts for power, engaged also in more serious struggles for safety against the fierce tribes of the unconverted Frisians, Bavarians, Saxons, and Thuringians, who at that epoch assailed with peculiar ferocity the christianized Germans on the left bank of the Rhine,

Charles Martel added experienced skill to his natural courage, and he had also formed a militia of veterans among the Franks. Hallam has thrown out a doubt whether, in our admiration of his victory at Tours, we do not judge a little too much by the event, and whether there was not rashness in his risking the fate of France on the result of a general battle with the invaders. But, when we remember that Charles had no standing army, and the independent spirit of the Frank warriors who followed his standard, it seems most probable that it was not in his power to adopt the cautious policy of watching the invaders, and wearing out their strength by delay. So dreadful and so wide-spread were the ravages of the Saracenic light cavalry throughout Gaul that it must have been impossible to restrain for any length of time the indignant ardour of the Franks. And, even if Charles could have persuaded his men to look tamely on while the Arabs stormed more towns and desolated more districts, he could not have kept an army together when the usual period of a military expedition had expired. If, indeed, the Arab account of the disorganization of the Moslem forces be correct, the battle was as well-timed on the part of Charles as it was beyond all question, well-fought.

The monkish chroniclers, from whom we are obliged to glean a narrative of this memorable campaign, bear full evidence to the terror which the Saracen invasion inspired, and to the agony of that; great struggle. The Saracens, say they, and their king, who was called Abdirames, came out of Spain, with all their wives, and their children, and their substance, in such great multitudes that no man could reckon or estimate them. They brought with them all their armour, and whatever they had, as if they were thence forth always to dwell in France.

"Then Abderrahman, seeing the land filled with the multitude of his army, pierces through the mountains, tramples over rough and level ground plunders far into the country of the Franks, and smites all with the sword, insomuch that when Eudo came to battle with him at the river Garonne, and fled before him, God alone knows the number of the slain. Then Abderrahman pursued after Count Eudo, and while he strives to spoil and burn the holy shrine at Tours, he encounters the chief of the Austrasian Franks, Charles, a man of war from his youth up, to whom Eudo had sent warning. There for nearly seven days they strive intensely, and at last they set themselves in battle array; and the nations of the north standing firm as a wall, and impenetrable as a zone of ice, utterly slay the Arabs with the edge of the sword."

The European writers all concur in speaking of the fall of Abderrahman as one of the principal causes of the defeat of the Arabs; who, according to one writer, after finding that their leader was slain, dispersed in the night, to the agreeable surprise of the Christians, who expected the next morning to see them issue from their tents, and renew the combat. One monkish chronicler puts the loss of the Arabs at 375,000 men, while he says that only 1,007 Christians fell--a disparity of loss which he feels bound to account for by a special interposition of Providence. I have translated above some of the most spirited passages of these writers; but it is impossible to collect from them anything like a full or authentic description of the great battle itself, or of the operations which preceded or followed it.

Though, however, we may have cause to regret the meagreness and doubtful character of these narratives, we have the great advantage of being able to compare the accounts given of Abderrahman's expedition by the national writers of each side. This is a benefit which the inquirer into antiquity so seldom can obtain, that the fact of possessing it, in the instance of the battle of Tours, makes us think the historical testimony respecting that great event more certain and satisfactory than is the case in many other instances, where we possess abundant details respecting military exploits, but where those details come to us from the annalist of one nation only; and where we have, consequently, no safeguard against the exaggerations, the distortions, and the fictions which national vanity has so often put forth in the garb and under the title of history.

The Arabian writers who recorded the conquests and wars of their countrymen in Spain, have narrated also the expedition into Gaul of their great Emir, and his defeat and death near Tours in battle with the host of the Franks under King Caldus, the name into which they metamorphose Charles.

They tell us how there was war between the count of the Frankish frontier and the Moslems, and how the count gathered together all his people, and fought for a time with doubtful success. "But," say the Arabian chroniclers, "Abderrahman drove them back; and the men of Abderrahman were puffed up in spirit by their repeated successes, and they were full of trust in the valour and the practice in war of their Emir. So the Moslems smote their enemies, and passed the river Garonne, and laid waste the country, and took captives without number. And that army went through all places like a desolating storm. Prosperity made those warriors insatiable. At the passage of the river, Abderrahman overthrew the count, and the count retired into his stronghold, but the Moslems fought against it, and entered it by force, and slew the count; for everything gave way to their scimetars, which were the robbers of lives. All the nations of the Franks trembled at that terrible army, and they betook them to their king Caldus, and told him of the havoc made by the Moslem horsemen, and how they rode at their will through all the land of Narbonne Toulouse, and Bordeaux, and they told the king of the death of their count. Then the king bade them be of good cheer, and offered to aid them. And in the 114th year he mounted his home, and he took with him a host that could not be numbered, and went against the Moslems. And he came upon them at the great city of Tours. And Abderrahman and other prudent cavaliers saw the disorder of the Moslem troops, who were loaded with spoil; but they did not venture to displease the soldiers by ordering them to abandon everything except their arms and war-horses. And Abderrahman trusted in the valour of his soldiers, and in the good fortune which had ever attended him. But (the Arab writer remarks) such defect of discipline always is fatal to armies. So Abderrahman and his host attacked Tours to gain still more spoil, and they fought against it so fiercely that they stormed the city almost before the eyes of the army that came to save it; and the fury and the cruelty of the Moslems towards the inhabitants of the city were like the fury and cruelty of raging tigers. It was manifest," adds the Arab, "that God's chastisement was sure to follow such excesses; and fortune thereupon turned her back upon the Moslems.

"Near the river Owar, the two great hosts of the two languages and the two creeds were set in array against each other. The hearts of Abderrahman, his captains, and his men were filled with wrath and pride, and they were the first to begin the fight. The Moslem horseman dashed fierce and frequent forward against the battalions of the Franks, who resisted manfully, and many fell dead on either side, until the going down of the sun. Night parted the two armies: but in the grey of the morning the Moslems returned to the battle. Their cavaliers had soon hewn their way into the centre of the Christian host. But many of the Moslems were fearful for the safety of the spoil which they had stored in their tents, and a false cry arose in their ranks that some of the enemy were plundering the camp; whereupon several squadrons of the Moslem horseman rode off to protect their tents. But it seemed as if they fled; and all the host was troubled. And while Abderrahman strove to check their tumult, and to lead them back to battle, the warriors of the Franks came around him, and he was pierced through with many spears, so that he died. Then all the host fled before the enemy, and many died in the flight. This deadly defeat of the Moslems, and the loss of the great leader and good cavalier Abderrahman, took place in the hundred and fifteenth year.

It would be difficult to expect from an adversary a more explicit confession of having been thoroughly vanquished, than the Arabs here accord to the Europeans. The points on which their narrative differs from those of the Christians, - as to how many days the conflict lasted, whether the assailed city was actually rescued or not, and the like, - are of little moment compared with the admitted great fact that there was a decisive trial of strength between Frank and Saracen, in which the former conquered.

The enduring importance of the battle of Tours in the eyes of the Moslems, is attested not only by the expressions of "the deadly battle," and "the disgraceful overthrow," which their writers constantly employ when referring to it, but also by the fact that no further serious attempts at conquest beyond the Pyrenees were made by the Saracens. Charles Martel, and his son and grandson, were left at leisure to consolidate and extend their power. The new Christian Roman Empire of the West, which the genius of Charlemagne founded, and throughout which his iron will imposed peace on the old anarchy of creeds and races, did not indeed retain its integrity after its great ruler's death. Fresh troubles came over Europe; but Christendom, though disunited, was safe. The progress of civilization, and the development of the nationalities and governments of modern Europe, from that time forth, went forward in not uninterrupted, but, ultimately, certain career.

Synopsis of Events Between the Battle of Tours, A.D. 732, and the Battle of Hastings, 1066.

768-814 - Reign of Charlemagne. This monarch has justly been termed the principal regenerator of Western Europe, after the destruction of the Roman empire. The early death of his brother, Carloman, left him sole master of the dominions of the Franks, which, by a succession of victorious wars, he enlarged into the new Empire of the West.

He conquered the Lombards, and re-established the Pope at Rome, who, in return, acknowledged Charles as suzerain of Italy. and in the year 800, Leo III, in the name of the Roman people, solemnly crowned Charlemagne at Rome, as

Emperor of the Roman Empire of the West. In Spain, Charlemagne ruled the country between the Pyrenees and the Ebro; but his most important conquests were effected on the eastern side of his original kingdom, over the Sclavonians of Bohemia, the Avars of Pannonia, and over the previously uncivilized German tribes who had remained in their fatherland. The old Saxons were his most obstinate antagonists, and his wars with them lasted for thirty years.

Under him the greater part of Germany was compulsorily civilized, and converted from Paganism to Christianity, His empire extended eastward as far as the Elbe, the Saal, the Bohemian mountains, and a line drawn from thence crossing the Danube above Vienna, and prolonged to the Gulf of Istria.

Throughout this vast assemblage of provinces, Charlemagne established an organized and firm government. But it is not as a mere conqueror that he demands admiration. "In a life restlessly active, we see him reforming the coinage, and establishing the legal divisions of money, gathering about him the learned of every country; founding schools and collecting libraries; interfering, with the air of a king, in religious controversies; attempting, for the sake of commerce, the magnificent enterprise of uniting the Rhine and the Danube, and meditating to mould the discordant code of Roman and barbarian laws into an uniform system."

814-888. Repeated partitions of the empire and civil wars between Charlemagne's descendants. Ultimately, the kingdom of France is finally separated from Germany and Italy. In 982, Otho the Great, of Germany, revives the imperial dignity.

827. Egbert, king of Wessex, acquires the supremacy over the Anglo-Saxon kingdoms.

832. The first Danish squadron attacks part of the English coast. The Danes, or Northmen, had begun their ravages in France a few years earlier. For two centuries Scandinavia sends out fleet after fleet of sea-rovers, who desolate all the

western kingdoms of Europe, and in many cases effect permanent conquests.

871-900. Reign of Alfred in England. After a long and varied struggle, he rescues England from the Danish invaders.

911. The French king cedes Neustria to Hrolf the Northman. Hrolf (or Duke Rollo, as he thenceforth was termed) and his army of Scandinavian warriors, become the ruling class of the population of the province, which is called after them Normandy.

1016. Four knights from Normandy, who had been on a pilgrimage to the Holy Land, while returning through Italy, head the people of Salerno in repelling an attack of a band of Saracen corsairs.

In the next year many adventurers from Normandy settle in Italy, where they conquer Apulia (1040), and afterwards (1060) Sicily.

1017. Canute, king of Denmark, becomes king of England. On the death of the last of his sons, in 1041, the Saxon line is restored, and Edward the Confessor (who had been bred in the court of the Duke of Normandy), is called by the English to the throne of this island, as the representative of the House of Cerdic.

1035. Duke Robert of Normandy dies on his return from a pilgrimage to the Holy

Land, and his son William (afterwards the conqueror of England) succeeds to the dukedom of Normandy.

Chapter IV

Who were the Franks [6]

During the reign of Charles Martel, the Franks kingdom was described as the foremost military power of Western Europe.

The name Franks seems to have been given in the 4th century to a group of Germanic peoples dwelling north of the Main and reaching as far as the shores of the North Sea; south of the Main was the home of the Alamanni. The names of some of these tribes have come down to us. On the *Tabula Peutingeriana* appear the "Chamavi qui et *Pranci*," which should doubtless read "qui et *Franci*"; these

---

[6] Based on the work of Christian Pfister.

Chamavi apparently dwelt between the Yssel and the Ems.

Later, we find them a little farther south, on the banks of the Rhine, in the district called Hamalant, and it is their customs which were brought together in the 9th century in the document known as the *Lex Francorum Chamavorum*. After the Chamavi we may mention the Attuarii or Chattuarii, who are referred to by Ammianus Marcellinus (xx. 10, 2): "Rheno exinde transmisso, regionem pervasit (Julianus) Francorum quos Atthuarios vocant." Later, the *pagus Attuariorum* corresponds to the district of Emmerich and Xanten. It should be noted that this name occurs again in the middle ages in Burgundy, not far from Dijon; in all probability a detachment of this people had settled in that spot in the 5th or 6th century. The Bructeri, Ampsivarii and Chatti may also be classed among the Frankish tribes. They are mentioned in a celebrated passage of Sulpicius Alexander, which is cited by Gregory of Tours (*Historia Francorum*, ii. 9). Sulpicius shows the general Arbogast, a barbarian in the service of Rome, seeking to take vengeance on the Franks (392): *"Collecto exercitu, transgressus Rhenum, Bricteros ripae proximos, pagum etiam quem Chamavi incolunt depopulatus est, nullo unquam occursante, nisi quod pauci ex Ampsivariis et Catthis Marcomere duce in ulterioribus collium jugis apparuere."*

It is evidently this Marcomeres, the chief of these tribes, who is regarded by later historians as the father of the legendary Faramund (Pharamund) although in fact Marcomeres has nothing to do with the Salian Franks.

The earliest mention in history of the name Franks is the entry on the *Tabula Peutingeriana*, at least if we assume that the term "et Franci" is not a later emendation. The earliest occurrence of the name in any author is in the *Vita Aureliani* of Vopiscus.

When, in 241, Aurelian, who was then only a tribune, had just defeated some Franks in the neighbourhood of Mainz and was marching against the Persians, his troops sang the following refrain:

> Mille Sarmatas, mille *Francos*, semel et semel occidimus;
> Mille Persas, quaerimus.

All these Germanic tribes, which were known from the 3rd century onwards by the generic name of Franks, doubtless spoke a similar dialect and were governed by customs which must scarcely have differed from one another; but this was all they had in common. Each tribe was politically independent; they formed no confederations. Sometimes two or three tribes joined forces to wage a war; but, the struggle over, the bond was broken, and each tribe resumed its isolated life. Waitz holds with some show of probability that the Franks represent the ancient Istaevones of Tacitus, the Alamanni and the Saxons representing the Herminones and the Ingaevones.

Of all these Frankish tribes one especially was to become prominent, the tribe of the Salians. They are mentioned for the first time in 358, by Ammianus Marcellinus, who says that the Caesar Julian "petit primos omnium Francos, videlicet eos quos consuetude Salios appellavit." As to the origin of the name, it was long held to be derived from the river Yssel or Saal. It is more probable, however, that it arose from the fact that the Salians for a long period occupied the shores of the salt sea. The Salians inhabited the sea-coast, whereas the Ripuarians dwelt on the banks of the river Rhine.

The Salians, at the time when they are mentioned by Ammianus, occupied Toxandria, *i.e.* the region south of the Meuse, between that river and the Scheldt. Julian defeated them completely, but allowed them to remain in Toxandria, not, as of old, as conquerors, but as *foederati* of the Romans. They perhaps paid tribute, and they certainly furnished Rome with soldiers; *Salii seniores* and *Salii juniores* are mentioned in the *Notitia dignitatum*, and Salii appear among the *auxilia palatina*.

At the end of the 4th century and at the beginning of the 5th, when the Roman legions withdrew from the banks of the Rhine, the Salians installed themselves in the district as an independent people. The place-names became entirely Germanic; the Latin language disappeared; and the Christian religion suffered a check, for the Franks were to a man pagans. The Salians were subdivided into a certain number of tribes, each tribe placing at its head a king, distinguished by his long hair and chosen from the most noble family (*Historia Francorum*).

The most ancient of these kings, reigning over the principal tribe, who is known to us is Chlodio. According to Gregory of Tours Chlodio dwelt at a place called Dispargum, which it is impossible to identify. Towards 431 he crossed the great Roman road from Bavay to Cologne, which was protected by numerous forts and had long arrested the invasions of the barbarians. He then invaded the territory of Arras, but was severely defeated at Hesdin-le-Vieux by Aetius, the commander of the Roman army in Gaul. Chlodio, however, soon took his revenge. He explored the region of Cambrai, seized that town, and occupied all the country as far as the

Somme. At this time Tournai became the capital of the Salian Franks.

After Chlodio a certain Meroveus (Merowech) was king of the Salian Franks. We do not know if he was the son of Chlodio; Gregory of Tours simply says that he belonged to Chlodio's stock — "de hujus stirpe quidam Merovechum regem fuisse adserunt," — and then only gives the fact at second hand. Perhaps the remarks of the Byzantine historian Priscus may refer to Meroveus. A king of the Franks having died, his two sons disputed the power. The elder journeyed into Pannonia to obtain support from Attila; the younger betook himself to the imperial court at Rome. "I have seen him," writes Priscus; "he was still very young, and we all remarked his fair hair which fell upon his shoulders."

Aetius welcomed him warmly and sent him back a friend and *foederatus*. In any case, eventually, Franks fought (451) in the Roman ranks at the great battle of Mauriac (the Catalaunian Fields), which arrested the progress of Attila into Gaul; and in the *Vita Lupi*, which, though undoubtedly of later date, is a recension of an earlier document, the name of Meroveus appears among the combatants. Towards 457 Meroveus was succeeded by his son Childeric. At first Childeric was a faithful *foederatus* of the Romans, fighting for them against the Visigoths and the Saxons south of the Loire; but he soon sought to make himself independent and to extend his conquests. He died in 481 and was succeeded by his son Clovis, who conquered the whole of Gaul with the exception of the kingdom of

Burgundy and Provence. Clovis made his authority recognized over the other Salian tribes (whose kings dwelt at Cambrai and other cities), and put an end to the domination of the Ripuarian Franks.

These Ripuarians must have comprised a certain number of Frankish tribes, such as the Ampsivarii and the Bructeri. They settled in the 5th century in compact masses on the left bank of the Rhine, but their progress was slow. It was not until the Christian writer Salvian (who was born about 400) had already reached a fairly advanced age that they were able to seize Cologne. The town, however, was recaptured and was not definitely in their possession until 463.

The Ripuarians subsequently occupied all the country from Cologne to Trier. Aix-la-Chapelle, Bonn and Zülpich were their principal centres, and they even advanced southward as far as Metz, which appears to have resisted their attacks. The Roman civilization and the Latin language disappeared from the countries which they occupied; indeed it seems that the actual boundaries of the German and French languages nearly coincide with those of their dominion. In their southward progress the Ripuarians encountered the Alamanni, who, already masters of Alsace, were endeavouring to extend their conquests in all directions. There were numerous battles between the Ripuarians and the Alamanni; and the memory of one fought at Zülpich has come down to us. In this battle Sigebert, the king of the Ripuarians, was wounded in the knee and limped during the remainder of his life — hence his surname Claudus (the Lame).

The Ripuarians long remained allies of Clovis, Sigebert's son Chloderic fighting under the king of the Salian Franks at Vouillé in 507. Clovis, however, persuaded Chloderic to assassinate his father, and then posed as Sigebert's avenger, with the result that Chloderic was himself assassinated and the Ripuarians raised Clovis on the shield and chose him as king. Thus the Salian Franks united under their rule all the Franks on the left bank of the Rhine. During the reigns of Clovis's sons they again turned their eyes on Germany, and imposed their suzerainty upon the Franks on the right bank. This country, north of the Main and the first residence of the Franks, then received the name of

Francia Orientalis, and became the origin of one of the duchies into which Germany was divided in the 10th century — the duchy of Franconia (Franken).

The Franks were redoubtable warriors, and were generally of great stature. Their fair or red hair was brought forward from the crown of the head towards the forehead, leaving the nape of the neck uncovered; they shaved the face except the upper lip. They wore fairly close breeches reaching to the knee and a tunic fastened by brooches. Round the waist over the tunic was worn a leathern girdle having a broad iron buckle damascened with silver. From the girdle hung the single-edged missile axe or *francisca*, the *scramasax* or short knife, a poniard and such articles of toilet as scissors, a comb (of wood or bone), &c. The Franks also used a weapon called the *framea* (an iron lance set firmly in a wooden shaft), and bows and arrows. They protected themselves in battle with a large wooden or wicker shield, the centre of which was ornamented with an iron boss (*umbo*). Frankish arms and armour have been found in the cemeteries which abound throughout northern France, the warriors being buried fully armed.

Conclusion

Charles Martel was twenty-five or twenty six years old when his father Pepin died in 714.

Nature had been most bountiful to Charles Martel : tall even among the tall nation of the Franks, of a most commanding figure, and of a compact and beautifully symmetrical frame, he might be said to present in his physical conformation a compound of Hercules and Antinous; his features were regular and expressive, and the lightning glance of his large blue eyes reflected, as in a mirror, the energy of his mind and the vigor of his intellect. He possessed enormous bodily strength combined with surprising agility. The remembrance of his great father, and his own manly beauty and grace, gained him the hearts of the Austrasians.

He was a brave young man. He had fought in many of his father's battles and so had become a skilled soldier. His men were devoted to him.

While he was mayor of the palace he led armies in several wars against the enemies of the Franks. The most important of his wars was one with the Saracens, who came across the Pyrenees from Spain and invaded the land of the Franks, intending to establish Mohammedanism there. Their army was led by Abd-er-Rahman, the Saracen governor of Spain.

On his march through the southern districts of the land of the Franks Abd-er-Rahman destroyed many towns and villages, killed a number of the people, and seized all the property he could carry off. He plundered the city of Bordeaux, and, it is said, obtained so many valuable things that every soldier "was loaded with golden vases and cups and emeralds and other precious stones."

But meanwhile Charles Martel was not idle. As quickly as he could he got together a great army of Franks and Germans and marched against the Saracens. The two armies met between the cities of Tours and Poitiers in October, 732. For six days there was nothing but an occasional skirmish between small parties from both sides; but on the seventh day a great battle took place.

Both Christians and Mohammedans fought with terrible earnestness. The fight went on all day, and the field was covered with the bodies of the slain. But towards evening, during a resolute charge made by the Franks, Abd-er-Rahman was killed. Then the Saracens gradually retired to their camp.

It was not yet known, however, which side had won; and the Franks expected that the fight would be renewed in the morning.

But when Charles Martel, with his Christian warriors, appeared on the field at sunrise there was no enemy to fight. The Mohammedans had fled in the silence and darkness of the night and had left behind them all their valuable spoils. There was now no doubt which side had won.

The battle of Tours, or Poitiers, as it should be called, is regarded as one of the decisive battles of the world. It decided that Christians, and not Moslems, should be the ruling power in Europe.

Charles Martel is especially celebrated as the hero of this battle. It is said that the name *Martel* was given to him because of his bravery during the fight. Marteau is the French word for hammer, and one of the old French historians says that as a hammer breaks and crushes iron and steel, so Charles broke and crushed the power of his enemies in the battle of Tours.

But though the Saracens fled from the battlefield of Tours, they did not leave the land of the Franks; and Charles had to fight other battles with them, before they were finally defeated. At last, however, he drove them across the Pyrenees, and they never again attempted to invade Frankland.

After his defeat of the Saracens Charles Martel was looked upon as the great champion of Christianity; and to the day of his death, in 741, he was in reality, though not in name, the king of the Franks.

Bibliography:

- Christian Pfister, *Charles Martel*. (Short biography)

- Christian Pfister, *The Franks*.

- Edward Shepherd Creasy in *The Fifteen Decisive Battles of the World*.

- Godefroid Kurth, *Charles Martel*.

- John H. Haaren, *Charles Martel and Pepin, (in Famous Men of the Middle Ages.)*

- Strauss G. L., in *Charles Martel and the Rescue of Europe from the threatened yoke of the Saracens*.

www.ingramcontent.com/pod-product-compliance
Lightning Source LLC
Chambersburg PA
CBHW031407040426
42444CB00005B/456